LORD BYRON POETRY COLLECTION

Table of Contents

Farewell

by Lord Byron

Farewell was written in 1808 as a farewell to his wife. It was published with Lord Byron's well received tale, The Corsair in 1814.

Farewell! if ever fondest prayer
　For other's weal availed on high,
Mine will not all be lost in air,
　But waft thy name beyond the sky,
'Twere vain to speak, to weep, to sigh:
　Oh! more than tears of blood can tell,
When wrung from guilt's expiring eye,
　Are in that word—Farewell!—Farewell!

These lips are mute, these eyes are dry;
　But in my breast, and in my brain,
Awake the pangs that pass not by,
　The thought that ne'er shall sleep again.
My soul nor deigns nor dares complain,
　Though grief and passion there rebel;
I only know we loved in vain—
　I only feel—Farewell!—Farewell!

THE END.

From the Turkish

by Lord Byron

From the Turkish was published in Byron's most popular tale, The Corsair in 1814.

1.

The chain I gave was fair to view,
   The lute I added sweet in sound,
The heart that offered both was true,
   And ill deserv'd the fate it found.

2.

These gifts were charm'd by secret spell
   Thy truth in absence to divine;
And they have done their duty well,
   Alas! they could not teach thee thine.

3.

That chain was firm in every link.
   But not to bear a stranger's touch;
That lute was sweet—till thou could'st think
   In other hands ts notes were such.

4.

Let him, who from thy neck unbound

The chain which shiver'd in his grasp,
Who saw that lute refuse to sound,
   Restring the chords, renew the clasp.

5.

When thou wert chang'd, they alter'd too;
   The chain is broke, the music mute:
'Tis past—to them and thee adieu—
   False heart, frail chain, and silent lute.

Inscription on the Monument of a Newfoundland Dog

by Lord Byron

Inscription on the Monument of a Newfoundland Dog, sometimes referred to as Epitaph to a Dog commemorates the life of Byron's dog, Boatswain. It was written in 1808 and published in Lord Byron's well received tale, The Corsair in 1814. The headstone for the cherished dog is bigger than Byron's own.

When some proud son of man returns to earth,
Unknown to glory, but upheld by birth,
The sculptor's art exhausts the pomp of woe,
And storied urns record who rests below;
When all is done, upon the tomb is seen,
Not what he was, but what he should have been:
But the poor dog, in life the firmest friend,
The first to welcome, foremost to defend,
Whose honest heart is still his master's own,
Who labours, fights, lives, breathes for him alone,
Unhonour'd falls, unnotic'd all his worth,
Denied in heaven the soul he held on earth:
While man, vain insect! hopes to be forgiven,
And claims himself a sole exclusive heaven.
Oh man! thou feeble tenant of an hour,
Debas'd by slavery, or corrupt by power,
Who knows thee well must quit thee with disgust,
Degraded mass of animated dust!
Thy love is lust, thy friendship all a cheat,
Thy smiles hypocrisy, thy words deceit!
By nature vile, ennobled but by name,

Each kindred brute might bid thee blush for shame.
Ye! who perchance behold this simple urn,
Pass on—it honours none you wish to mourn:
To mark a friend's remains these stones arise,
I never knew but one, and here he lies.

She Walks in Beauty

by Lord Byron

Byron composed this piece in 1813 after being
mesmerized by a lady dressed in black at a ball, his cousin
by marriage.

She walks in beauty, like the night
Of cloudless climes and starry skies;
And all that's best of dark and bright
Meet in her aspect and her eyes:
Thus mellow'd to that tender light
Which heaven to gaudy day denies.

One shade the more, one ray the less,
Had half impaired the nameless grace
Which waves in every raven tress,
Or softly lightens o'er her face;
Where thoughts serenely sweet express
How pure, how dear their dwelling-place.

And on that cheek, and o'er that brow,
So soft, so calm, yet eloquent,
The smiles that win, the tints that glow,
But tell of days in goodness spent,
A mind at peace with all below,
A heart whose love is innocent!

Sonnet I

by Lord Byron

Thine eyes blue tenderness, thy long fair hair,
　And the wan lustre of thy features—caught
　From contemplation—where serenely wrought,
Seems Sorrow's softness charm'd from its despair—
Have thrown such speaking sadness in thine air,
　That—but I know thy blessed bosom fraught
　With mines of unalloy'd and stainless thought—
I should have deem'd thee doom'd to earthly care.
With such an aspect by his colours blent,
　When from his beauty-breathing pencil born,
(Except that thou hast nothing to repent)
　The Magdalen of Guido saw the morn—
Such seem'st thou—but how much more excellent!
　With nought Remorse can claim—nor Virtue scorn.

Sonnet II

by Lord Byron

Sonnet II was published in Byron's most popular tale, The Corsair in 1814.

To Genevra.

Thy cheek is pale with thought, but not from woe,
☐And yet so lovely, that if Mirth could flush
☐Its rose of whiteness with the brightest blush,
My heart would wish away that ruder glow:—
And dazzle not thy deep-blue eyes—but oh!
☐While gazing on them sterner eyes will gush,
☐And into mine my mother's weakness rush,
Soft as the last drops round heaven's airy bow;
For, through thy long dark lashes low depending,
☐The soul of melancholy Gentleness
Gleams like a seraph from the sky descending,
☐Above all pain, yet pitying all distress;
At once such majesty with sweetness blending,
☐I worship more, but cannot love thee less.

To a Lady Weeping

by Lord Byron

To a Lady Weeping was first published anonymously in the Morning Chronicle. It was later published with Byron's most popular tale, The Corsair in 1814. It references Princess Charlotte of Wales's reaction to her father, the Prince Regent (George IV, who would later be king) abandonment of his Whig supporters in favor of the Tories. Princess Charlotte would have been queen had she outlived George IV, but she died at age 21 during childbirth.

To a Lady weeping.

Weep, daughter of a royal line,
 A Sire's disgrace, a realm's decay;
Ah, happy! if each tear of thine
 Could wash a father's fault away!

Weep—for thy tears are Virtue's tears—
 Auspicious to these suffering isles;
And be each drop in future years
 Repaid thee by thy people's smiles!

March, 1812.

The Corsair

by Lord Byron

CANTO 1

Canto the First

"———nessun maggior dolore,
Che ricordarsi del tempo felice
Nella miseria,———"

Dante, Inferno, v. 121.

I.

"O'er the glad waters of the dark blue sea,
Our thoughts as boundless, and our souls as free,
Far as the breeze can bear, the billows foam,
Survey our empire, and behold our home!
These are our realms, no limits to their sway—
Our flag the sceptre all who meet obey.
Ours the wild life in tumult still to range
From toil to rest, and joy in every change.
Oh, who can tell? not thou, luxurious slave!
Whose soul would sicken o'er the heaving wave;
Not thou, vain lord of Wantonness and Ease!
Whom Slumber soothes not—Pleasure cannot please—
Oh, who can tell, save he whose heart hath tried,

And danced in triumph o'er the waters wide,
The exulting sense—the pulse's maddening play,
That thrills the wanderer of that trackless way?
That for itself can woo the approaching fight,
And turn what some deem danger to delight;
That seeks what cravens shun with more than zeal,
And where the feebler faint can only feel— ☐
Feel—to the rising bosom's inmost core,
Its hope awaken and its spirit soar?
No dread of Death—if with us die our foes—
Save that it seems even duller than repose;
Come when it will—we snatch the life of Life—
When lost—what recks it by disease or strife?
Let him who crawls, enamoured of decay,
Cling to his couch, and sicken years away;
Heave his thick breath, and shake his palsied head;
Ours the fresh turf, and not the feverish bed,— ☐
While gasp by gasp he falters forth his soul,
Ours with one pang—one bound—escapes control.
His corse may boast its urn and narrow cave,
And they who loathed his life may gild his grave:
Ours are the tears, though few, sincerely shed,
When Ocean shrouds and sepulchres our dead.
For us, even banquets fond regret supply
In the red cup that crowns our memory;
And the brief epitaph in Danger's day,
When those who win at length divide the prey, ☐
And cry, Remembrance saddening o'er each brow,
How had the brave who fell exulted now!"

II.

Such were the notes that from the Pirate's isle

13

Around the kindling watch-fire rang the while:
Such were the sounds that thrilled the rocks along,
And unto ears as rugged seemed a song!
In scattered groups upon the golden sand,
They game—carouse—converse—or whet the brand;
Select the arms—to each his blade assign,
And careless eye the blood that dims its shine; ☐
Repair the boat, replace the helm or oar,
While others straggling muse along the shore;
For the wild bird the busy springes set,
Or spread beneath the sun the dripping net:
Gaze where some distant sail a speck supplies,
With all the thirsting eye of Enterprise;
Tell o'er the tales of many a night of toil,
And marvel where they next shall seize a spoil:
No matter where—their chief's allotment this;
Theirs to believe no prey nor plan amiss. ☐
But who that Chief? his name on every shore
Is famed and feared—they ask and know no more.
With these he mingles not but to command;
Few are his words, but keen his eye and hand.
Ne'er seasons he with mirth their jovial mess,
But they forgive his silence for success.
Ne'er for his lip the purpling cup they fill,
That goblet passes him untasted still—
And for his fare—the rudest of his crew
Would that, in turn, have passed untasted too; ☐
Earth's coarsest bread, the garden's homeliest roots,
And scarce the summer luxury of fruits,
His short repast in humbleness supply
With all a hermit's board would scarce deny.
But while he shuns the grosser joys of sense,
His mind seems nourished by that abstinence.
"Steer to that shore!"—they sail. "Do this!"—'tis done:

"Now form and follow me!"—the spoil is won.
Thus prompt his accents and his actions still,
And all obey and few inquire his will; □
To such, brief answer and contemptuous eye
Convey reproof, nor further deign reply.

III.

"A sail!—a sail!"—a promised prize to Hope!
Her nation—flag—how speaks the telescope?
No prize, alas! but yet a welcome sail:
The blood-red signal glitters in the gale.
Yes—she is ours—a home-returning bark—
Blow fair, thou breeze!—she anchors ere the dark.
Already doubled is the cape—our bay
Receives that prow which proudly spurns the spray. □
How gloriously her gallant course she goes!
Her white wings flying—never from her foes—
She walks the waters like a thing of Life,
And seems to dare the elements to strife.
Who would not brave the battle-fire, the wreck,
To move the monarch of her peopled deck!

IV.

Hoarse o'er her side the rustling cable rings:
The sails are furled; and anchoring round she swings;
And gathering loiterers on the land discern
Her boat descending from the latticed stern. □
'Tis manned—the oars keep concert to the strand,

Till grates her keel upon the shallow sand.
Hail to the welcome shout!—the friendly speech!
When hand grasps hand uniting on the beach;
The smile, the question, and the quick reply,
And the Heart's promise of festivity!

V.

The tidings spread, and gathering grows the crowd:
The hum of voices, and the laughter loud,
And Woman's gentler anxious tone is heard—
Friends'—husbands'—lovers' names in each dear word:
"Oh! are they safe? we ask not of success—
But shall we see them? will their accents bless?
From where the battle roars, the billows chafe,
They doubtless boldly did—but who are safe?
Here let them haste to gladden and surprise,
And kiss the doubt from these delighted eyes!"

VI.

"Where is our Chief? for him we bear report—
And doubt that joy—which hails our coming—short;
Yet thus sincere—'tis cheering, though so brief;
But, Juan! instant guide us to our Chief:
Our greeting paid, we'll feast on our return,
And all shall hear what each may wish to learn."
Ascending slowly by the rock-hewn way,
To where his watch-tower beetles o'er the bay,
By bushy brake, the wild flowers blossoming,

And freshness breathing from each silver spring,
Whose scattered streams from granite basins burst,
Leap into life, and sparkling woo your thirst;
From crag to cliff they mount—Near yonder cave,
What lonely straggler looks along the wave? ☐
In pensive posture leaning on the brand,
Not oft a resting-staff to that red hand?
"'Tis he—'tis Conrad—here—as wont—alone;
On—Juan!—on—and make our purpose known.
The bark he views—and tell him we would greet
His ear with tidings he must quickly meet:
We dare not yet approach—thou know'st his mood,
When strange or uninvited steps intrude."

VII.

Him Juan sought, and told of their intent;—
He spake not, but a sign expressed assent, ☐
These Juan calls—they come—to their salute
He bends him slightly, but his lips are mute.
"These letters, Chief, are from the Greek—the spy,
Who still proclaims our spoil or peril nigh:
Whate'er his tidings, we can well report,
Much that"—"Peace, peace!"—he cuts their prating short.
Wondering they turn, abashed, while each to each
Conjecture whispers in his muttering speech:
They watch his glance with many a stealing look,
To gather how that eye the tidings took; ☐
But, this as if he guessed, with head aside,
Perchance from some emotion, doubt, or pride,
He read the scroll—"My tablets, Juan, hark—
Where is Gonsalvo?"

"In the anchored bark."
"There let him stay—to him this order bear—
Back to your duty—for my course prepare:
Myself this enterprise to-night will share."
"To-night, Lord Conrad?"
"Aye! at set of sun:
The breeze will freshen when the day is done.
My corslet—cloak—one hour and we are gone.
Sling on thy bugle—see that free from rust
My carbine-lock springs worthy of my trust;
Be the edge sharpened of my boarding-brand,
And give its guard more room to fit my hand.
This let the Armourer with speed dispose;
Last time, it more fatigued my arm than foes;
Mark that the signal-gun be duly fired,
To tell us when the hour of stay's expired."

VIII.

They make obeisance, and retire in haste,
Too soon to seek again the watery waste:
Yet they repine not—so that Conrad guides;
And who dare question aught that he decides?
That man of loneliness and mystery,
Scarce seen to smile, and seldom heard to sigh;
Whose name appals the fiercest of his crew,
And tints each swarthy cheek with sallower hue;
Still sways their souls with that commanding art
That dazzles, leads, yet chills the vulgar heart.
What is that spell, that thus his lawless train
Confess and envy—yet oppose in vain?
What should it be, that thus their faith can bind?

18

The power of Thought—the magic of the Mind!
Linked with success, assumed and kept with skill,
That moulds another's weakness to its will;
Wields with their hands, but, still to these unknown,
Makes even their mightiest deeds appear his own.
Such hath it been—shall be—beneath the Sun
The many still must labour for the one!
'Tis Nature's doom—but let the wretch who toils,
Accuse not—hate not—him who wears the spoils. ☐
Oh! if he knew the weight of splendid chains,
How light the balance of his humbler pains!

IX.

Unlike the heroes of each ancient race,
Demons in act, but Gods at least in face,
In Conrad's form seems little to admire,
Though his dark eyebrow shades a glance of fire:
Robust but not Herculean—to the sight
No giant frame sets forth his common height;
Yet, in the whole, who paused to look again,
Saw more than marks the crowd of vulgar men; ☐
They gaze and marvel how—and still confess
That thus it is, but why they cannot guess.
Sun-burnt his cheek, his forehead high and pale
The sable curls in wild profusion veil;
And oft perforce his rising lip reveals
The haughtier thought it curbs, but scarce conceals.
Though smooth his voice, and calm his general mien,
Still seems there something he would not have seen:
His features' deepening lines and varying hue
At times attracted, yet perplexed the view, ☐

As if within that murkiness of mind
Worked feelings fearful, and yet undefined;
Such might it be—that none could truly tell—
Too close inquiry his stern glance would quell.
There breathe but few whose aspect might defy
The full encounter of his searching eye;
He had the skill, when Cunning's gaze would seek
To probe his heart and watch his changing cheek,
At once the observer's purpose to espy,
And on himself roll back his scrutiny,☐220
Lest he to Conrad rather should betray
Some secret thought, than drag that Chief's to day.
There was a laughing Devil in his sneer,
That raised emotions both of rage and fear;
And where his frown of hatred darkly fell,
Hope withering fled—and Mercy sighed farewell!

X.[10]

Slight are the outward signs of evil thought,
Within—within—'twas there the spirit wrought!
Love shows all changes—Hate, Ambition, Guile,
Betray no further than the bitter smile;☐
The lip's least curl, the lightest paleness thrown
Along the governed aspect, speak alone
Of deeper passions; and to judge their mien,
He, who would see, must be himself unseen.
Then—with the hurried tread, the upward eye,
The clenchéd hand, the pause of agony,
That listens, starting, lest the step too near
Approach intrusive on that mood of fear:
Then—with each feature working from the heart,

With feelings, loosed to strengthen—not depart,☐
That rise—convulse—contend—that freeze or glow,
Flush in the cheek, or damp upon the brow;
Then—Stranger! if thou canst, and tremblest not,
Behold his soul—the rest that soothes his lot!
Mark how that lone and blighted bosom sears
The scathing thought of execrated years!
Behold—but who hath seen, or e'er shall see,
Man as himself—the secret spirit free?

XI.

Yet was not Conrad thus by Nature sent
To lead the guilty—Guilt's worst instrument—☐
His soul was changed, before his deeds had driven
Him forth to war with Man and forfeit Heaven.
Warped by the world in Disappointment's school,
In words too wise—in conduct there a fool;
Too firm to yield, and far too proud to stoop,
Doomed by his very virtues for a dupe,
He cursed those virtues as the cause of ill,
And not the traitors who betrayed him still;
Nor deemed that gifts bestowed on better men
Had left him joy, and means to give again.☐
Feared—shunned—belied—ere Youth had lost her force,
He hated Man too much to feel remorse,
And thought the voice of Wrath a sacred call,
To pay the injuries of some on all.
He knew himself a villain—but he deemed
The rest no better than the thing he seemed;
And scorned the best as hypocrites who hid
Those deeds the bolder spirit plainly did.

He knew himself detested, but he knew
The hearts that loathed him, crouched and dreaded too.
Lone, wild, and strange, he stood alike exempt
From all affection and from all contempt:
His name could sadden, and his acts surprise;
But they that feared him dared not to despise:
Man spurns the worm, but pauses ere he wake
The slumbering venom of the folded snake:
The first may turn, but not avenge the blow;
The last expires, but leaves no living foe;
Fast to the doomed offender's form it clings,
And he may crush—not conquer—still it stings!

XII.

None are all evil—quickening round his heart,
One softer feeling would not yet depart;
Oft could he sneer at others as beguiled
By passions worthy of a fool or child;
Yet 'gainst that passion vainly still he strove,
And even in him it asks the name of Love!
Yes, it was love—unchangeable—unchanged,
Felt but for one from whom he never ranged;
Though fairest captives daily met his eye,
He shunned, nor sought, but coldly passed them by;
Though many a beauty drooped in prisoned bower,
None ever soothed his most unguarded hour.
Yes—it was Love—if thoughts of tenderness,
Tried in temptation, strengthened by distress,
Unmoved by absence, firm in every clime,
And yet—Oh more than all!—untired by Time;
Which nor defeated hope, nor baffled wile,

Could render sullen were She near to smile,
Nor rage could fire, nor sickness fret to vent
On her one murmur of his discontent;☐
Which still would meet with joy, with calmness part,
Lest that his look of grief should reach her heart;
Which nought removed, nor menaced to remove—
If there be Love in mortals—this was Love!
He was a villain—aye, reproaches shower
On him—but not the Passion, nor its power,
Which only proved—all other virtues gone—
Not Guilt itself could quench this loveliest one!

XIII.

He paused a moment—till his hastening men
Passed the first winding downward to the glen.☐
"Strange tidings!—many a peril have I passed,
Nor know I why this next appears the last!
Yet so my heart forebodes, but must not fear,
Nor shall my followers find me falter here.
'Tis rash to meet—but surer death to wait
Till here they hunt us to undoubted fate;
And, if my plan but hold, and Fortune smile,
We'll furnish mourners for our funeral pile.
Aye, let them slumber—peaceful be their dreams!
Morn ne'er awoke them with such brilliant beams☐
As kindle high to-night (but blow, thou breeze!)
To warm these slow avengers of the seas.
Now to Medora—Oh! my sinking heart,
Long may her own be lighter than thou art!
Yet was I brave—mean boast where all are brave!
Ev'n insects sting for aught they seek to save.

This common courage which with brutes we share,
That owes its deadliest efforts to Despair,
Small merit claims—but 'twas my nobler hope
To teach my few with numbers still to cope;□
Long have I led them—not to vainly bleed:
No medium now—we perish or succeed!
So let it be—it irks not me to die;
But thus to urge them whence they cannot fly.
My lot hath long had little of my care,
But chafes my pride thus baffled in the snare:
Is this my skill? my craft? to set at last
Hope, Power and Life upon a single cast?
Oh, Fate!—accuse thy folly—not thy fate;
She may redeem thee still—nor yet too late."□

XIV.

Thus with himself communion held he, till
He reached the summit of his tower-crowned hill:
There at the portal paused—for wild and soft
He heard those accents never heard too oft!
Through the high lattice far yet sweet they rung,
And these the notes his Bird of Beauty sung:

1.

"Deep in my soul that tender secret dwells,
□Lonely and lost to light for evermore,
Save when to thine my heart responsive swells,
□Then trembles into silence as before.□

2.

"There, in its centre, a sepulchral lamp
  Burns the slow flame, eternal—but unseen;
Which not the darkness of Despair can damp,
  Though vain its ray as it had never been.

3.

"Remember me—Oh! pass not thou my grave
  Without one thought whose relics there recline:
The only pang my bosom dare not brave
  Must be to find forgetfulness in thine.

4.

"My fondest—faintest—latest accents hear—
  Grief for the dead not Virtue can reprove;
Then give me all I ever asked—a tear,
  The first—last—sole reward of so much love!"

He passed the portal, crossed the corridor,
And reached the chamber as the strain gave o'er:
"My own Medora! sure thy song is sad—"

"In Conrad's absence would'st thou have it glad?
Without thine ear to listen to my lay,
Still must my song my thoughts, my soul betray:
Still must each accent to my bosom suit,
My heart unhushed—although my lips were mute!
Oh! many a night on this lone couch reclined,

My dreaming fear with storms hath winged the wind,
And deemed the breath that faintly fanned thy sail
The murmuring prelude of the ruder gale;
Though soft—it seemed the low prophetic dirge,
That mourned thee floating on the savage surge:
Still would I rise to rouse the beacon fire,
Lest spies less true should let the blaze expire;
And many a restless hour outwatched each star,
And morning came—and still thou wert afar.
Oh! how the chill blast on my bosom blew,
And day broke dreary on my troubled view,
And still I gazed and gazed—and not a prow
Was granted to my tears—my truth—my vow!
At length—'twas noon—I hailed and blest the mast
That met my sight—it neared—Alas! it passed!
Another came—Oh God! 'twas thine at last!
Would that those days were over! wilt thou ne'er,
My Conrad! learn the joys of peace to share?
Sure thou hast more than wealth, and many a home
As bright as this invites us not to roam:
Thou know'st it is not peril that I fear,
I only tremble when thou art not here;
Then not for mine, but that far dearer life,
Which flies from love and languishes for strife—
How strange that heart, to me so tender still,
Should war with Nature and its better will!"

"Yea, strange indeed—that heart hath long been changed;
Worm-like 'twas trampled—adder-like avenged—
Without one hope on earth beyond thy love,
And scarce a glimpse of mercy from above.
Yet the same feeling which thou dost condemn,
My very love to thee is hate to them,

So closely mingling here, that disentwined,
I cease to love thee when I love Mankind:
Yet dread not this—the proof of all the past
Assures the future that my love will last;
But—Oh, Medora! nerve thy gentler heart;
This hour again—but not for long—we part."

"This hour we part!—my heart foreboded this:☐
Thus ever fade my fairy dreams of bliss.
This hour—it cannot be—this hour away!
Yon bark hath hardly anchored in the bay:
Her consort still is absent, and her crew
Have need of rest before they toil anew;
My Love! thou mock'st my weakness; and wouldst steel
My breast before the time when it must feel;
But trifle now no more with my distress,
Such mirth hath less of play than bitterness.
Be silent, Conrad!—dearest! come and share☐
The feast these hands delighted to prepare;
Light toil! to cull and dress thy frugal fare!
See, I have plucked the fruit that promised best,
And where not sure, perplexed, but pleased, I guessed
At such as seemed the fairest; thrice the hill
My steps have wound to try the coolest rill;
Yes! thy Sherbet to-night will sweetly flow,
See how it sparkles in its vase of snow!
The grape's gay juice thy bosom never cheers;
Thou more than Moslem when the cup appears:☐
Think not I mean to chide—for I rejoice
What others deem a penance is thy choice.
But come, the board is spread; our silver lamp
Is trimmed, and heeds not the Sirocco's damp:
Then shall my handmaids while the time along,

And join with me the dance, or wake the song;
Or my guitar, which still thou lov'st to hear,
Shall soothe or lull—or, should it vex thine ear,
We'll turn the tale, by Ariosto told,
Of fair Olympia loved and left of old.
Why, thou wert worse than he who broke his vow
To that lost damsel, should thou leave me now—
Or even that traitor chief—I've seen thee smile,
When the clear sky showed Ariadne's Isle,
Which I have pointed from these cliffs the while:
And thus half sportive—half in fear—I said,
Lest Time should raise that doubt to more than dread,
Thus Conrad, too, will quit me for the main:
And he deceived me—for—he came again!"

"Again, again—and oft again—my Love! □
If there be life below, and hope above,
He will return—but now, the moments bring
The time of parting with redoubled wing:
The why, the where—what boots it now to tell?
Since all must end in that wild word—Farewell!
Yet would I fain—did time allow—disclose—
Fear not—these are no formidable foes!
And here shall watch a more than wonted guard,
For sudden siege and long defence prepared:
Nor be thou lonely, though thy Lord's away, □
Our matrons and thy handmaids with thee stay;
And this thy comfort—that, when next we meet,
Security shall make repose more sweet.
List!—'tis the bugle!"—Juan shrilly blew—
"One kiss—one more—another—Oh! Adieu!"
She rose—she sprung—she clung to his embrace,
Till his heart heaved beneath her hidden face:

He dared not raise to his that deep-blue eye,
Which downcast drooped in tearless agony.
Her long fair hair lay floating o'er his arms, ☐
In all the wildness of dishevelled charms;
Scarce beat that bosom where his image dwelt
So full—that feeling seem'd almost unfelt!
Hark—peals the thunder of the signal-gun!
It told 'twas sunset, and he cursed that sun.
Again—again—that form he madly pressed,
Which mutely clasped, imploringly caressed!
And tottering to the couch his bride he bore,
One moment gazed—as if to gaze no more;
Felt that for him Earth held but her alone, ☐
Kissed her cold forehead—turned—is Conrad gone?

XV.

"And is he gone?"—on sudden solitude
How oft that fearful question will intrude!
"'Twas but an instant past, and here he stood!
And now"—without the portal's porch she rushed,
And then at length her tears in freedom gushed;
Big, bright, and fast, unknown to her they fell;
But still her lips refused to send—"Farewell!"
For in that word—that fatal word—howe'er
We promise—hope—believe—there breathes Despair.
O'er every feature of that still, pale face, ☐
Had Sorrow fixed what Time can ne'er erase:
The tender blue of that large loving eye
Grew frozen with its gaze on vacancy,
Till—Oh, how far!—it caught a glimpse of him,
And then it flowed, and phrensied seemed to swim

Through those long, dark, and glistening lashes dewed
With drops of sadness oft to be renewed.
"He's gone!"—against her heart that hand is driven,
Convulsed and quick—then gently raised to Heaven: ☐
She looked and saw the heaving of the main;
The white sail set—she dared not look again;
But turned with sickening soul within the gate—
"It is no dream—and I am desolate!"

XVI.

From crag to crag descending, swiftly sped
Stern Conrad down, nor once he turned his head;
But shrunk whene'er the windings of his way
Forced on his eye what he would not survey,
His lone, but lovely dwelling on the steep,
That hailed him first when homeward from the deep:
And she—the dim and melancholy Star, ☐
Whose ray of Beauty reached him from afar,
On her he must not gaze, he must not think—
There he might rest—but on Destruction's brink:
Yet once almost he stopped—and nearly gave
His fate to chance, his projects to the wave:
But no—it must not be—a worthy chief
May melt, but not betray to Woman's grief.
He sees his bark, he notes how fair the wind,
And sternly gathers all his might of mind: ☐
Again he hurries on—and as he hears
The clang of tumult vibrate on his ears,
The busy sounds, the bustle of the shore,
The shout, the signal, and the dashing oar;
As marks his eye the seaboy on the mast,

The anchors rise, the sails unfurling fast,
The waving kerchiefs of the crowd that urge
That mute Adieu to those who stem the surge;
And more than all, his blood-red flag aloft,
He marvelled how his heart could seem so soft. ☐
Fire in his glance, and wildness in his breast,
He feels of all his former self possest;
He bounds—he flies—until his footsteps reach
The verge where ends the cliff, begins the beach,
There checks his speed; but pauses less to breathe
The breezy freshness of the deep beneath,
Than there his wonted statelier step renew;
Nor rush, disturbed by haste, to vulgar view:
For well had Conrad learned to curb the crowd,
By arts that veil, and oft preserve the proud; ☐
His was the lofty port, the distant mien,
That seems to shun the sight—and awes if seen:
The solemn aspect, and the high-born eye,
That checks low mirth, but lacks not courtesy;
All these he wielded to command assent:
But where he wished to win, so well unbent,
That Kindness cancelled fear in those who heard,
And others' gifts showed mean beside his word,
When echoed to the heart as from his own
His deep yet tender melody of tone: ☐
But such was foreign to his wonted mood,
He cared not what he softened, but subdued;
The evil passions of his youth had made
Him value less who loved—than what obeyed.

XVII.

31

Around him mustering ranged his ready guard.
Before him Juan stands—"Are all prepared?"
"They are—nay more—embarked: the latest boat
Waits but my chief——"
☐"My sword, and my capote."
Soon firmly girded on, and lightly slung,
His belt and cloak were o'er his shoulders flung:☐
"Call Pedro here!" He comes—and Conrad bends,
With all the courtesy he deigned his friends;
"Receive these tablets, and peruse with care,
Words of high trust and truth are graven there;
Double the guard, and when Anselmo's bark
Arrives, let him alike these orders mark:
In three days (serve the breeze) the sun shall shine
On our return—till then all peace be thine!"
This said, his brother Pirate's hand he wrung,
Then to his boat with haughty gesture sprung.☐
Flashed the dipt oars, and sparkling with the stroke,
Around the waves' phosphoric[20] brightness broke;
They gain the vessel—on the deck he stands,—
Shrieks the shrill whistle, ply the busy hands—
He marks how well the ship her helm obeys,
How gallant all her crew, and deigns to praise.
His eyes of pride to young Gonsalvo turn—
Why doth he start, and inly seem to mourn?
Alas! those eyes beheld his rocky tower,
And live a moment o'er the parting hour;☐
She—his Medora—did she mark the prow?
Ah! never loved he half so much as now!
But much must yet be done ere dawn of day—
Again he mans himself and turns away;
Down to the cabin with Gonsalvo bends,
And there unfolds his plan—his means, and ends;
Before them burns the lamp, and spreads the chart,

And all that speaks and aids the naval art;
They to the midnight watch protract debate;
To anxious eyes what hour is ever late? □
Meantime, the steady breeze serenely blew,
And fast and falcon-like the vessel flew;
Passed the high headlands of each clustering isle,
To gain their port—long—long ere morning smile:
And soon the night-glass through the narrow bay
Discovers where the Pacha's galleys lay.
Count they each sail, and mark how there supine
The lights in vain o'er heedless Moslem shine.
Secure, unnoted, Conrad's prow passed by,
And anchored where his ambush meant to lie; □
Screened from espial by the jutting cape,
That rears on high its rude fantastic shape.
Then rose his band to duty—not from sleep—
Equipped for deeds alike on land or deep;
While leaned their Leader o'er the fretting flood,
And calmly talked—and yet he talked of blood!

CANTO II

Canto the Second

"Conosceste i dubbiosi desiri?"

Dante, Inferno, v. 120.

I.

"In Coron's bay floats many a galley light,
Through Coron's lattices the lamps are bright,
For Seyd, the Pacha, makes a feast to-night:
A feast for promised triumph yet to come,
When he shall drag the fettered Rovers home;
This hath he sworn by Allah and his sword,
And faithful to his firman and his word,
His summoned prows collect along the coast,
And great the gathering crews, and loud the boast;
Already shared the captives and the prize,
Though far the distant foe they thus despise;
'Tis but to sail—no doubt to-morrow's Sun
Will see the Pirates bound—their haven won!
Meantime the watch may slumber, if they will,
Nor only wake to war, but dreaming kill.
Though all, who can, disperse on shore and seek
To flesh their glowing valour on the Greek;
How well such deed becomes the turbaned brave—
To bare the sabre's edge before a slave!
Infest his dwelling—but forbear to slay,
Their arms are strong, yet merciful to-day,

And do not deign to smite because they may!
Unless some gay caprice suggests the blow,
To keep in practice for the coming foe.□
Revel and rout the evening hours beguile,
And they who wish to wear a head must smile;
For Moslem mouths produce their choicest cheer,
And hoard their curses, till the coast is clear.

II.

High in his hall reclines the turbaned Seyd;
Around—the bearded chiefs he came to lead.
Removed the banquet, and the last pilaff—
Forbidden draughts, 'tis said, he dared to quaff
Though to the rest the sober berry's juice
The slaves bear round for rigid Moslems' use;□
The long chibouque's[3] dissolving cloud supply,
While dance the Almas[4] to wild minstrelsy.
The rising morn will view the chiefs embark;
But waves are somewhat treacherous in the dark:
And revellers may more securely sleep
On silken couch than o'er the rugged deep:
Feast there who can—nor combat till they must,
And less to conquest than to Korans trust;
And yet the numbers crowded in his host
Might warrant more than even the Pacha's boast.□

III.

With cautious reverence from the outer gate

Slow stalks the slave, whose office there to wait,
Bows his bent head—his hand salutes the floor,
Ere yet his tongue the trusted tidings bore:
"A captive Dervise, from the Pirate's nest
Escaped, is here—himself would tell the rest."
He took the sign from Seyd's assenting eye,
And led the holy man in silence nigh.
His arms were folded on his dark-green vest,
His step was feeble, and his look deprest;
Yet worn he seemed of hardship more than years,
And pale his cheek with penance, not from fears.
Vowed to his God—his sable locks he wore,
And these his lofty cap rose proudly o'er:
Around his form his loose long robe was thrown,
And wrapt a breast bestowed on heaven alone;
Submissive, yet with self-possession manned,
He calmly met the curious eyes that scanned;
And question of his coming fain would seek,
Before the Pacha's will allowed to speak.

IV.

"Whence com'st thou, Dervise?"
　"From the Outlaw's den
A fugitive—"
　"Thy capture where and when?"
"From Scalanova's port[6] to Scio's isle.
The Saick[7] was bound; but Allah did not smile
Upon our course—the Moslem merchant's gains
The Rovers won; our limbs have worn their chains.
I had no death to fear, nor wealth to boast,
Beyond the wandering freedom which I lost;

At length a fisher's humble boat by night
Afforded hope, and offered chance of flight; ☐
I seized the hour, and find my safety here—
With thee—most mighty Pacha! who can fear?"

"How speed the outlaws? stand they well prepared,
Their plundered wealth, and robber's rock, to guard?
Dream they of this our preparation, doomed
To view with fire their scorpion nest consumed?"

"Pacha! the fettered captive's mourning eye,
That weeps for flight, but ill can play the spy;
I only heard the reckless waters roar,
Those waves that would not bear me from the shore; ☐
I only marked the glorious Sun and sky,
Too bright—too blue—for my captivity;
And felt that all which Freedom's bosom cheers
Must break my chain before it dried my tears.
This mayst thou judge, at least, from my escape,
They little deem of aught in Peril's shape;
Else vainly had I prayed or sought the chance
That leads me here—if eyed with vigilance:
The careless guard that did not see me fly,
May watch as idly when thy power is nigh. ☐
Pacha! my limbs are faint—and nature craves
Food for my hunger, rest from tossing waves:
Permit my absence—peace be with thee! Peace
With all around!—now grant repose—release."

"Stay, Dervise! I have more to question—stay,
I do command thee—sit—dost hear?—obey!

More I must ask, and food the slaves shall bring;
Thou shalt not pine where all are banqueting:
The supper done—prepare thee to reply,
Clearly and full—I love not mystery."□
'Twere vain to guess what shook the pious man,
Who looked not lovingly on that Divan;
Nor showed high relish for the banquet prest,
And less respect for every fellow guest.
'Twas but a moment's peevish hectic passed
Along his cheek, and tranquillised as fast:
He sate him down in silence, and his look
Resumed the calmness which before forsook:
The feast was ushered in—but sumptuous fare
He shunned as if some poison mingled there.□
For one so long condemned to toil and fast,
Methinks he strangely spares the rich repast.
"What ails thee, Dervise? eat—dost thou suppose
This feast a Christian's? or my friends thy foes?
Why dost thou shun the salt? that sacred pledge,
Which, once partaken, blunts the sabre's edge,
Makes even contending tribes in peace unite,
And hated hosts seem brethren to the sight!"

"Salt seasons dainties—and my food is still
The humblest root, my drink the simplest rill;□
And my stern vow and Order's[9] laws oppose
To break or mingle bread with friends or foes;
It may seem strange—if there be aught to dread
That peril rests upon my single head;
But for thy sway—nay more—thy Sultan's throne,
I taste nor bread nor banquet—save alone;
Infringed our Order's rule, the Prophet's rage
To Mecca's dome might bar my pilgrimage."

"Well—as thou wilt—ascetic as thou art—
One question answer; then in peace depart.☐
How many?—Ha! it cannot sure be day?
What Star—what Sun is bursting on the bay?
It shines a lake of fire!—away—away!
Ho! treachery! my guards! my scimitar!
The galleys feed the flames—and I afar!
Accurséd Dervise!—these thy tidings—thou
Some villain spy—seize—cleave him—slay him now!"

Up rose the Dervise with that burst of light,
Nor less his change of form appalled the sight:
Up rose that Dervise—not in saintly garb,☐
But like a warrior bounding on his barb,
Dashed his high cap, and tore his robe away—
Shone his mailed breast, and flashed his sabre's ray!
His close but glittering casque, and sable plume,
More glittering eye, and black brow's sabler gloom,
Glared on the Moslems' eyes some Afrit Sprite,
Whose demon death-blow left no hope for fight.
The wild confusion, and the swarthy glow
Of flames on high, and torches from below;
The shriek of terror, and the mingling yell—☐
For swords began to clash, and shouts to swell—
Flung o'er that spot of earth the air of Hell!
Distracted, to and fro, the flying slaves
Behold but bloody shore and fiery waves;
Nought heeded they the Pacha's angry cry,
They seize that Dervise!—seize on Zatanai!
He saw their terror—checked the first despair
That urged him but to stand and perish there,

Since far too early and too well obeyed,
The flame was kindled ere the signal made;☐
He saw their terror—from his baldric drew
His bugle—brief the blast—but shrilly blew;
'Tis answered—"Well ye speed, my gallant crew!
Why did I doubt their quickness of career?
And deem design had left me single here?"
Sweeps his long arm—that sabre's whirling sway
Sheds fast atonement for its first delay;
Completes his fury, what their fear begun,
And makes the many basely quail to one.
The cloven turbans o'er the chamber spread,☐
And scarce an arm dare rise to guard its head:
Even Seyd, convulsed, o'erwhelmed, with rage, surprise,
Retreats before him, though he still defies.
No craven he—and yet he dreads the blow,
So much Confusion magnifies his foe!
His blazing galleys still distract his sight,
He tore his beard, and foaming fled the fight;
For now the pirates passed the Haram gate,
And burst within—and it were death to wait;
Where wild Amazement shrieking—kneeling—throws
The sword aside—in vain—the blood o'erflows!☐
The Corsairs pouring, haste to where within
Invited Conrad's bugle, and the din
Of groaning victims, and wild cries for life,
Proclaimed how well he did the work of strife.
They shout to find him grim and lonely there,
A glutted tiger mangling in his lair!
But short their greeting, shorter his reply—
"'Tis well—but Seyd escapes—and he must die—
Much hath been done—but more remains to do—☐
Their galleys blaze—why not their city too?"

V.

Quick at the word they seized him each a torch,
And fire the dome from minaret to porch.
A stern delight was fixed in Conrad's eye,
But sudden sunk—for on his ear the cry
Of women struck, and like a deadly knell
Knocked at that heart unmoved by Battle's yell.
"Oh! burst the Haram—wrong not on your lives
One female form—remember—we have wives.
On them such outrage Vengeance will repay; □
Man is our foe, and such 'tis ours to slay:
But still we spared—must spare the weaker prey.
Oh! I forgot—but Heaven will not forgive
If at my word the helpless cease to live;
Follow who will—I go—we yet have time
Our souls to lighten of at least a crime."
He climbs the crackling stair—he bursts the door,
Nor feels his feet glow scorching with the floor;
His breath choked gasping with the volumed smoke,
But still from room to room his way he broke. □
They search—they find—they save: with lusty arms
Each bears a prize of unregarded charms;
Calm their loud fears; sustain their sinking frames
With all the care defenceless Beauty claims:
So well could Conrad tame their fiercest mood,
And check the very hands with gore imbrued.
But who is she? whom Conrad's arms convey,
From reeking pile and combat's wreck, away—
Who but the love of him he dooms to bleed?
The Haram queen—but still the slave of Seyd! □

41

VI.

Brief time had Conrad now to greet Gulnare,
Few words to reassure the trembling Fair;
For in that pause Compassion snatched from War,
The foe before retiring, fast and far,
With wonder saw their footsteps unpursued,
First slowlier fled—then rallied—then withstood.
This Seyd perceives, then first perceives how few,
Compared with his, the Corsair's roving crew,
And blushes o'er his error, as he eyes
The ruin wrought by Panic and Surprise.□
Alla il Alla! Vengeance swells the cry—
Shame mounts to rage that must atone or die!
And flame for flame and blood for blood must tell,
The tide of triumph ebbs that flowed too well—
When Wrath returns to renovated strife,
And those who fought for conquest strike for life.
Conrad beheld the danger—he beheld
His followers faint by freshening foes repelled:
"One effort—one—to break the circling host!"
They form—unite—charge—waver—all is lost!□
Within a narrower ring compressed, beset,
Hopeless, not heartless, strive and struggle yet—
Ah! now they fight in firmest file no more,
Hemmed in—cut off—cleft down and trampled o'er;
But each strikes singly—silently—and home,
And sinks outwearied rather than o'ercome—
His last faint quittance rendering with his breath,
Till the blade glimmers in the grasp of Death!

VII.

But first, ere came the rallying host to blows,
And rank to rank, and hand to hand oppose, □
Gulnare and all her Haram handmaids freed,
Safe in the dome of one who held their creed,
By Conrad's mandate safely were bestowed,
And dried those tears for life and fame that flowed:
And when that dark-eyed lady, young Gulnare,
Recalled those thoughts late wandering in despair,
Much did she marvel o'er the courtesy
That smoothed his accents, softened in his eye—
'Twas strange—that robber thus with gore bedewed,
Seemed gentler then than Seyd in fondest mood. □
The Pacha wooed as if he deemed the slave
Must seem delighted with the heart he gave;
The Corsair vowed protection, soothed affright,
As if his homage were a Woman's right.
"The wish is wrong—nay, worse for female—vain:
Yet much I long to view that Chief again;
If but to thank for, what my fear forgot,
The life—my loving Lord remembered not!"

VIII.

And him she saw, where thickest carnage spread,
But gathered breathing from the happier dead; □
Far from his band, and battling with a host
That deem right dearly won the field he lost,
Felled—bleeding—baffled of the death he sought,
And snatched to expiate all the ills he wrought;

Preserved to linger and to live in vain,
While Vengeance pondered o'er new plans of pain,
And stanched the blood she saves to shed again—
But drop by drop, for Seyd's unglutted eye
Would doom him ever dying—ne'er to die!
Can this be he? triumphant late she saw,☐
When his red hand's wild gesture waved, a law!
'Tis he indeed—disarmed but undeprest,
His sole regret the life he still possest;
His wounds too slight, though taken with that will,
Which would have kissed the hand that then could kill.
Oh were there none, of all the many given,
To send his soul—he scarcely asked to Heaven?
Must he alone of all retain his breath,
Who more than all had striven and struck for death?
He deeply felt—what mortal hearts must feel,☐
When thus reversed on faithless Fortune's wheel,
For crimes committed, and the victor's threat
Of lingering tortures to repay the debt—
He deeply, darkly felt; but evil Pride
That led to perpetrate—now serves to hide.
Still in his stern and self-collected mien
A conqueror's more than captive's air is seen,
Though faint with wasting toil and stiffening wound,
But few that saw—so calmly gazed around:
Though the far shouting of the distant crowd,☐
Their tremors o'er, rose insolently loud,
The better warriors who beheld him near,
Insulted not the foe who taught them fear;
And the grim guards that to his durance led,
In silence eyed him with a secret dread.

IX.

The Leech was sent—but not in mercy—there,
To note how much the life yet left could bear;
He found enough to load with heaviest chain,
And promise feeling for the wrench of Pain;
To-morrow—yea—to-morrow's evening Sun
Will, sinking, see Impalement's pangs begun,
And rising with the wonted blush of morn
Behold how well or ill those pangs are borne.
Of torments this the longest and the worst,
Which adds all other agony to thirst,
That day by day Death still forbears to slake,
While famished vultures flit around the stake.
"Oh! water—water!"—smiling Hate denies
The victim's prayer, for if he drinks he dies.
This was his doom;—the Leech, the guard, were gone,
And left proud Conrad fettered and alone.

X.

'Twere vain to paint to what his feelings grew —
It even were doubtful if their victim knew.
There is a war, a chaos of the mind,
When all its elements convulsed, combined
Lie dark and jarring with perturbéd force,
And gnashing with impenitent Remorse—
That juggling fiend, who never spake before,
But cries "I warned thee!" when the deed is o'er.
Vain voice! the spirit burning but unbent,
May writhe—rebel—the weak alone repent!
Even in that lonely hour when most it feels,

45

And, to itself, all—all that self reveals,—
No single passion, and no ruling thought
That leaves the rest, as once, unseen, unsought,
But the wild prospect when the Soul reviews,
All rushing through their thousand avenues—
Ambition's dreams expiring, Love's regret,
Endangered Glory, Life itself beset;
The joy untasted, the contempt or hate☐
'Gainst those who fain would triumph in our fate;
The hopeless past, the hasting future driven
Too quickly on to guess if Hell or Heaven;
Deeds—thoughts—and words, perhaps remembered not
So keenly till that hour, but ne'er forgot;
Things light or lovely in their acted time,
But now to stern Reflection each a crime;
The withering sense of Evil unrevealed,
Not cankering less because the more concealed;
All, in a word, from which all eyes must start,☐
That opening sepulchre, the naked heart
Bares with its buried woes—till Pride awake,
To snatch the mirror from the soul, and break.
Aye, Pride can veil, and Courage brave it all—
All—all—before—beyond—the deadliest fall.
Each hath some fear, and he who least betrays,
The only hypocrite deserving praise:
Not the loud recreant wretch who boasts and flies;
But he who looks on Death—and silent dies:
So, steeled by pondering o'er his far career,☐
He half-way meets Him should He menace near!

XI.

46

In the high chamber of his highest tower
Sate Conrad, fettered in the Pacha's power.
His palace perished in the flame—this fort
Contained at once his captive and his court.
Not much could Conrad of his sentence blame,
His foe, if vanquished, had but shared the same:—
Alone he sate—in solitude had scanned
His guilty bosom, but that breast he manned:
One thought alone he could not—dared not meet—☐
"Oh, how these tidings will Medora greet?"
Then—only then—his clanking hands he raised,
And strained with rage the chain on which he gazed;
But soon he found, or feigned, or dreamed relief,
And smiled in self-derision of his grief,
"And now come Torture when it will, or may—
More need of rest to nerve me for the day!"
This said, with langour to his mat he crept,
And, whatso'er his visions, quickly slept.

'Twas hardly midnight when that fray begun,☐
For Conrad's plans matured, at once were done,
And Havoc loathes so much the waste of time,
She scarce had left an uncommitted crime.
One hour beheld him since the tide he stemmed—
Disguised—discovered—conquering—ta'en—
condemned—
A Chief on land—an outlaw on the deep—
Destroying—saving—prisoned—and asleep!

XII.

47

He slept in calmest seeming, for his breath
Was hushed so deep—Ah! happy if in death!
He slept—Who o'er his placid slumber bends? □
His foes are gone—and here he hath no friends;
Is it some Seraph sent to grant him grace?
No, 'tis an earthly form with heavenly face!
Its white arm raised a lamp—yet gently hid,
Lest the ray flash abruptly on the lid,
Of that closed eye, which opens but to pain,
And once unclosed—but once may close again.
That form, with eye so dark, and cheek so fair,
And auburn waves of gemmed and braided hair;
With shape of faiiy lightness—naked foot, □
That shines like snow, and falls on earth as mute—
Through guards and dunnest night how came it there?
Ah! rather ask what will not Woman dare?
Whom Youth and Pity lead like thee, Gulnare!
She could not sleep—and while the Pacha's rest
In muttering dreams yet saw his pirate-guest,
She left his side—his signet-ring she bore,
Which oft in sport adorned her hand before—
And with it, scarcely questioned, won her way
Through drowsy guards that must that sign obey. □
Worn out with toil, and tired with changing blows,
Their eyes had envied Conrad his repose;
And chill and nodding at the turret door,
They stretch their listless limbs, and watch no more;
Just raised their heads to hail the signet-ring,
Nor ask or what or who the sign may bring.

XIII.

She gazed in wonder, "Can he calmly sleep,
While other eyes his fall or ravage weep?
And mine in restlessness are wandering here—
What sudden spell hath made this man so dear?
True—'tis to him my life, and more, I owe,
And me and mine he spared from worse than woe:
'Tis late to think—but soft—his slumber breaks—
How heavily he sighs!—he starts—awakes!"
He raised his head, and dazzled with the light,
His eye seemed dubious if it saw aright:
He moved his hand—the grating of his chain
Too harshly told him that he lived again.
"What is that form? if not a shape of air,
Methinks, my jailor's face shows wondrous fair!"
"Pirate! thou know'st me not, but I am one,
Grateful for deeds thou hast too rarely done;
Look on me—and remember her, thy hand
Snatched from the flames, and thy more fearful band.
I come through darkness—and I scarce know why—
Yet not to hurt—I would not see thee die."

"If so, kind lady! thine the only eye
That would not here in that gay hope delight:
Theirs is the chance—and let them use their right.
But still I thank their courtesy or thine,
That would confess me at so fair a shrine!"

Strange though it seem—yet with extremest grief
Is linked a mirth—it doth not bring relief—
That playfulness of Sorrow ne'er beguiles,
And smiles in bitterness—but still it smiles;
And sometimes with the wisest and the best,

Till even the scaffold[17] echoes with their jest!
Yet not the joy to which it seems akin—
It may deceive all hearts, save that within.
Whate'er it was that flashed on Conrad, now☐
A laughing wildness half unbent his brow:
And these his accents had a sound of mirth,
As if the last he could enjoy on earth;
Yet 'gainst his nature—for through that short life,
Few thoughts had he to spare from gloom and strife.

XIV.

"Corsair! thy doom is named—but I have power
To soothe the Pacha in his weaker hour.
Thee would I spare—nay more—would save thee now,
But this—Time—Hope—nor even thy strength allow;
But all I can,—I will—at least delay☐
The sentence that remits thee scarce a day.
More now were ruin—even thyself were loth
The vain attempt should bring but doom to both."

"Yes!—loth indeed:—my soul is nerved to all,
Or fall'n too low to fear a further fall:
Tempt not thyself with peril—me with hope
Of flight from foes with whom I could not cope:
Unfit to vanquish—shall I meanly fly,
The one of all my band that would not die?
Yet there is one—to whom my Memory clings,☐1080
Till to these eyes her own wild softness springs.
My sole resources in the path I trod
Were these—my bark—my sword—my love—my God!
The last I left in youth!—He leaves me now—

And Man but works his will to lay me low.
I have no thought to mock his throne with prayer
Wrung from the coward crouching of Despair;
It is enough—I breathe—and I can bear.
My sword is shaken from the worthless hand
That might have better kept so true a brand;□
My bark is sunk or captive—but my Love—
For her in sooth my voice would mount above:
Oh! she is all that still to earth can bind—
And this will break a heart so more than kind,
And blight a form—till thine appeared, Gulnare!
Mine eye ne'er asked if others were as fair."
"Thou lov'st another then?—but what to me
Is this—'tis nothing—nothing e'er can be:
But yet—thou lov'st—and—Oh! I envy those
Whose hearts on hearts as faithful can repose,□
Who never feel the void—the wandering thought
That sighs o'er visions—such as mine hath wrought."

"Lady—methought thy love was his, for whom
This arm redeemed thee from a fiery tomb."

"My love stern Seyd's! Oh—No—No—not my love—
Yet much this heart, that strives no more, once strove
To meet his passion—but it would not be.
I felt—I feel—Love dwells with—with the free.
I am a slave, a favoured slave at best,
To share his splendour, and seem very blest!□
Oft must my soul the question undergo,
Of—'Dost thou love?' and burn to answer, 'No!'
Oh! hard it is that fondness to sustain,
And struggle not to feel averse in vain;

But harder still the heart's recoil to bear,
And hide from one—perhaps another there.
He takes the hand I give not—nor withhold—
Its pulse nor checked—nor quickened—calmly cold:
And when resigned, it drops a lifeless weight
From one I never loved enough to hate.
No warmth these lips return by his imprest,
And chilled Remembrance shudders o'er the rest.
Yes—had I ever proved that Passion's zeal,
The change to hatred were at least to feel:
But still—he goes unmourned—returns unsought—
And oft when present—absent from my thought.
Or when Reflection comes—and come it must—
I fear that henceforth 'twill but bring disgust;
I am his slave—but, in despite of pride,
'Twere worse than bondage to become his bride.
Oh! that this dotage of his breast would cease!
Or seek another and give mine release,
But yesterday—I could have said, to peace!
Yes, if unwonted fondness now I feign,
Remember—Captive! 'tis to break thy chain;
Repay the life that to thy hand I owe;
To give thee back to all endeared below,
Who share such love as I can never know.
Farewell—Morn breaks—and I must now away:
'Twill cost me dear—but dread no death to-day!"

XV.

She pressed his fettered fingers to her heart,
And bowed her head, and turned her to depart,
And noiseless as a lovely dream is gone.

And was she here? and is he now alone?
What gem hath dropped and sparkles o'er his chain?
The tear most sacred, shed for others' pain,
That starts at once—bright—pure—from Pity's mine,
Already polished by the hand divine!
Oh! too convincing—dangerously dear—
In Woman's eye the unanswerable tear! □
That weapon of her weakness she can wield,
To save, subdue—at once her spear and shield:
Avoid it—Virtue ebbs and Wisdom errs,
Too fondly gazing on that grief of hers
What lost a world, and bade a hero fly?
The timid tear in Cleopatra's eye.
Yet be the soft Triumvir's fault forgiven;
By this—how many lose not earth—but Heaven!
Consign their souls to Man's eternal foe,
And seal their own to spare some Wanton's woe! □

XVI.

'Tis Morn—and o'er his altered features play
The beams—without the Hope of yesterday.
What shall he be ere night? perchance a thing
O'er which the raven flaps her funeral wing,
By his closed eye unheeded and unfelt;
While sets that Sun, and dews of Evening melt,
Chill, wet, and misty round each stiffened limb,
Refreshing earth—reviving all but him!

CANTO III

Canto the Third

"Come vedi—ancor non m'abbandona."

Dante, Inferno, v. 105.

I.

"Slow sinks, more lovely ere his race be run,
Along Morea's hills the setting Sun; ☐1170
Not, as in Northern climes, obscurely bright,
But one unclouded blaze of living light!
O'er the hushed deep the yellow beam he throws,
Gilds the green wave, that trembles as it glows.
On old Ægina's rock, and Idra's isle,
The God of gladness sheds his parting smile;
O'er his own regions lingering, loves to shine,
Though there his altars are no more divine.
Descending fast the mountain shadows kiss
Thy glorious gulf, unconquered Salamis! ☐
Their azure arches through the long expanse
More deeply purpled met his mellowing glance,
And tenderest tints, along their summits driven,
Mark his gay course, and own the hues of Heaven;
Till, darkly shaded from the land and deep,
Behind his Delphian cliff he sinks to sleep.

On such an eve, his palest beam he cast,
When—Athens! here thy Wisest looked his last.
How watched thy better sons his farewell ray,
That closed their murdered Sage's[3] latest day! ☐

54

Not yet—not yet—Sol pauses on the hill—
The precious hour of parting lingers still;
But sad his light to agonising eyes,
And dark the mountain's once delightful dyes:
Gloom o'er the lovely land he seemed to pour,
The land, where Phœbus never frowned before:
But ere he sunk below Cithæron's head,
The cup of woe was quaffed—the Spirit fled;
The Soul of him who scorned to fear or fly—
Who lived and died, as none can live or die!□

But lo! from high Hymettus to the plain,
The Queen of night asserts her silent reign.
No murky vapour, herald of the storm,
Hides her fair face, nor girds her glowing form;
With cornice glimmering as the moon-beams play,
There the white column greets her grateful ray,
And bright around with quivering beams beset,
Her emblem sparkles o'er the Minaret:
The groves of olive scattered dark and wide
Where meek Cephisus pours his scanty tide;□
The cypress saddening by the sacred Mosque,
The gleaming turret of the gay Kiosk;
And, dun and sombre 'mid the holy calm,
Near Theseus' fane yon solitary palm,
All tinged with varied hues arrest the eye—
And dull were his that passed them heedless by.

Again the Ægean, heard no more afar,
Lulls his chafed breast from elemental war;
Again his waves in milder tints unfold
Their long array of sapphire and of gold,□

Mixed with the shades of many a distant isle,
That frown—where gentler Ocean seems to smile.

II.

Not now my theme—why turn my thoughts to thee?
Oh! who can look along thy native sea.
Nor dwell upon thy name, whate'er the tale,
So much its magic must o'er all prevail?
Who that beheld that Sun upon thee set,
Fair Athens! could thine evening face forget?
Not he—whose heart nor time nor distance frees,
Spell-bound within the clustering Cyclades!
Nor seems this homage foreign to its strain,
His Corsair's isle was once thine own domain—
Would that with freedom it were thine again!

III.

The Sun hath sunk—and, darker than the night,
Sinks with its beam upon the beacon height
Medora's heart—the third day's come and gone—
With it he comes not—sends not—faithless one!
The wind was fair though light! and storms were none.
Last eve Anselmo's bark returned, and yet
His only tidings that they had not met!
Though wild, as now, far different were the tale
Had Conrad waited for that single sail.
The night-breeze freshens—she that day had passed
In watching all that Hope proclaimed a mast;

Sadly she sate on high—Impatience bore
At last her footsteps to the midnight shore,
And there she wandered, heedless of the spray
That dashed her garments oft, and warned away:
She saw not, felt not this—nor dared depart,
Nor deemed it cold—her chill was at her heart; □
Till grew such certainty from that suspense—
His very Sight had shocked from life or sense!

It came at last—a sad and shattered boat,
Whose inmates first beheld whom first they sought;
Some bleeding—all most wretched—these the few—
Scarce knew they how escaped—this all they knew.
In silence, darkling, each appeared to wait
His fellow's mournful guess at Conrad's fate:
Something they would have said; but seemed to fear
To trust their accents to Medora's ear. □
She saw at once, yet sunk not—trembled not—
Beneath that grief, that loneliness of lot,
Within that meek fair form, were feelings high,
That deemed not till they found their energy.
While yet was Hope they softened, fluttered, wept—
All lost—that Softness died not—but it slept;
And o'er its slumber rose that Strength which said,
"With nothing left to love, there's nought to dread."
'Tis more than Nature's—like the burning might
Delirium gathers from the fever's height. □

"Silent you stand—nor would I hear you tell
What—speak not—breathe not—for I know it well—
Yet would I ask—almost my lip denies
The—quick your answer—tell me where he lies."

"Lady! we know not—scarce with life we fled;
But here is one denies that he is dead:
He saw him bound; and bleeding—but alive."

She heard no further—'twas in vain to strive—
So throbbed each vein—each thought—till then
withstood;
Her own dark soul—these words at once subdued: ☐
She totters—falls—and senseless had the wave
Perchance but snatched her from another grave;
But that with hands though rude, yet weeping eyes,
They yield such aid as Pity's haste supplies:
Dash o'er her deathlike cheek the ocean dew,
Raise, fan, sustain—till life returns anew;
Awake her handmaids, with the matrons leave
That fainting form o'er which they gaze and grieve;
Then seek Anselmo's cavern, to report
The tale too tedious—when the triumph short. ☐

IV.

In that wild council words waxed warm and strange,
With thoughts of ransom, rescue, and revenge;
All, save repose or flight: still lingering there
Breathed Conrad's spirit, and forbade despair;
Whate'er his fate—the breasts he formed and led
Will save him living, or appease him dead.
Woe to his foes! there yet survive a few,
Whose deeds are daring, as their hearts are true.

V.

Within the Haram's secret chamber sate
Stem Seyd, still pondering o'er his Captive's fate;□
His thoughts on love and hate alternate dwell,
Now with Gulnare, and now in Conrad's cell;
Here at his feet the lovely slave reclined
Surveys his brow—would soothe his gloom of mind;
While many an anxious glance her large dark eye
Sends in its idle search for sympathy,
His only bends in seeming o'er his beads,
But inly views his victim as he bleeds.
"Pacha! the day is thine; and on thy crest
Sits Triumph—Conrad taken—fall'n the rest!□
His doom is fixed—he dies; and well his fate
Was earned—yet much too worthless for thy hate:
Methinks, a short release, for ransom told
With all his treasure, not unwisely sold;
Report speaks largely of his pirate-hoard—
Would that of this my Pacha were the lord!
While baffled, weakened by this fatal fray—
Watched—followed—he were then an easier prey;
But once cut off—the remnant of his band
Embark their wealth, and seek a safer strand."□

"Gulnare!—if for each drop of blood a gem
Were offered rich as Stamboul's diadem;
If for each hair of his a massy mine
Of virgin ore should supplicating shine;
If all our Arab tales divulge or dream

Of wealth were here—that gold should not redeem!
It had not now redeemed a single hour,
But that I know him fettered, in my power;
And, thirsting for revenge, I ponder still
On pangs that longest rack—and latest kill." □

"Nay, Seyd! I seek not to restrain thy rage,
Too justly moved for Mercy to assuage;
My thoughts were only to secure for thee
His riches—thus released, he were not free:
Disabled—shorn of half his might and band,
His capture could but wait thy first command."

"His capture could!—and shall I then resign
One day to him—the wretch already mine?
Release my foe!—at whose remonstrance?—thine!
Fair suitor!—to thy virtuous gratitude, □
That thus repays this Giaour's relenting mood,
Which thee and thine alone of all could spare—
No doubt, regardless—if the prize were fair—
My thanks and praise alike are due—now hear!
I have a counsel for thy gentler ear:
I do mistrust thee, Woman! and each word
Of thine stamps truth on all Suspicion heard.
Borne in his arms through fire from yon Serai—
Say, wert thou lingering there with him to fly?
Thou need'st not answer—thy confession speaks, □
Already reddening on thy guilty cheeks:
Then—lovely Dame—bethink thee! and beware:
'Tis not his life alone may claim such care!
Another word and—nay—I need no more.
Accurséd was the moment when he bore
Thee from the flames, which better far—but no—

I then had mourned thee with a lover's woe—
Now 'tis thy lord that warns—deceitful thing!
Know'st thou that I can clip thy wanton wing?
In words alone I am not wont to chafe:☐
Look to thyself—nor deem thy falsehood safe!"

He rose—and slowly, sternly thence withdrew,
Rage in his eye, and threats in his adieu:
Ah! little recked that Chief of womanhood—
Which frowns ne'er quelled, nor menaces subdued,
And little deemed he what thy heart, Gulnare!
When soft could feel—and when incensed could dare!
His doubts appeared to wrong—nor yet she knew
How deep the root from whence Compassion grew—
She was a slave—from such may captives claim☐
A fellow-feeling, differing but in name;
Still half unconscious—heedless of his wrath,
Again she ventured on the dangerous path,
Again his rage repelled—until arose
That strife of thought, the source of Woman's woes!

VI.

Meanwhile—long—anxious—weary—still the same
Rolled day and night: his soul could Terror tame—
This fearful interval of doubt and dread,
When every hour might doom him worse than dead;
When every step that echoed by the gate,☐
Might entering lead where axe and stake await;
When every voice that grated on his ear
Might be the last that he could ever hear;

Could Terror tame—that Spirit stern and high
Had proved unwilling as unfit to die;
'Twas worn—perhaps decayed—yet silent bore
That conflict, deadlier far than all before:
The heat of fight, the hurry of the gale,
Leave scarce one thought inert enough to quail:
But bound and fixed in fettered solitude, □
To pine, the prey of every changing mood;
To gaze on thine own heart—and meditate
Irrevocable faults, and coming fate—
Too late the last to shun—the first to mend—
To count the hours that struggle to thine end,
With not a friend to animate and tell
To other ears that Death became thee well;
Around thee foes to forge the ready lie,
And blot Life's latest scene with calumny;
Before thee tortures, which the Soul can dare, □
Yet doubts how well the shrinking flesh may bear;
But deeply feels a single cry would shame,
To Valour's praise thy last and dearest claim;
The life thou leav'st below, denied above
By kind monopolists of heavenly love;
And more than doubtful Paradise—thy Heaven
Of earthly hope—thy loved one from thee riven.
Such were the thoughts that outlaw must sustain,
And govern pangs surpassing mortal pain:
And those sustained he—boots it well or ill? □
Since not to sink beneath, is something still!

VII.

The first day passed—he saw not her—Gulnare—

The second, third—and still she came not there;
But what her words avouched, her charms had done,
Or else he had not seen another Sun.
The fourth day rolled along, and with the night
Came storm and darkness in their mingling might.
Oh! how he listened to the rushing deep,
That ne'er till now so broke upon his sleep;
And his wild Spirit wilder wishes sent, □
Roused by the roar of his own element!
Oft had he ridden on that wingéd wave,
And loved its roughness for the speed it gave;
And now its dashing echoed on his ear,
A long known voice—alas! too vainly near!
Loud sung the wind above; and, doubly loud,
Shook o'er his turret cell the thunder-cloud;
And flashed the lightning by the latticed bar,
To him more genial than the Midnight Star:
Close to the glimmering grate he dragged his chain, □
And hoped that peril might not prove in vain.
He rais'd his iron hand to Heaven, and prayed
One pitying flash to mar the form it made:
His steel and impious prayer attract alike—
The storm rolled onward, and disdained to strike;
Its peal waxed fainter—ceased—he felt alone,
As if some faithless friend had spurned his groan!

VIII.

The midnight passed, and to the massy door
A light step came—it paused—it moved once more;
Slow turns the grating bolt and sullen key: □
'Tis as his heart foreboded—that fair She!
Whate'er her sins, to him a Guardian Saint,

63

And beauteous still as hermit's hope can paint;
Yet changed since last within that cell she came,
More pale her cheek, more tremulous her frame:
On him she cast her dark and hurried eye,
Which spoke before her accents—"Thou must die!
Yes, thou must die—there is but one resource,
The last—the worst—if torture were not worse."

"Lady! I look to none; my lips proclaim☐
What last proclaimed they—Conrad still the same:
Why should'st thou seek an outlaw's life to spare,
And change the sentence I deserve to bear?
Well have I earned—nor here alone—the meed
Of Seyd's revenge, by many a lawless deed."

"Why should I seek? because—Oh! did'st thou not
Redeem my life from worse than Slavery's lot?
Why should I seek?—hath Misery made thee blind
To the fond workings of a woman's mind?
And must I say?—albeit my heart rebel☐
With all that Woman feels, but should not tell—
Because—despite thy crimes—that heart is moved:
It feared thee—thanked thee—pitied—maddened—loved.
Reply not, tell not now thy tale again,
Thou lov'st another—and I love in vain:
Though fond as mine her bosom, form more fair,
I rush through peril which she would not dare.
If that thy heart to hers were truly dear,
Were I thine own—thou wert not lonely here:
An outlaw's spouse—and leave her Lord to roam!☐
What hath such gentle dame to do with home?
But speak not now—o'er thine and o'er my head

Hangs the keen sabre by a single thread;
If thou hast courage still, and would'st be free,
Receive this poniard—rise and follow me!"

"Aye—in my chains! my steps will gently tread,
With these adornments, o'er such slumbering head!
Thou hast forgot—is this a garb for flight?
Or is that instrument more fit for fight?"

"Misdoubting Corsair! I have gained the guard,
Ripe for revolt, and greedy for reward.
A single word of mine removes that chain:
Without some aid how here could I remain?
Well, since we met, hath sped my busy time,
If in aught evil, for thy sake the crime:
The crime—'tis none to punish those of Seyd.
That hated tyrant, Conrad—he must bleed!
I see thee shudder, but my soul is changed—
Wronged—spurned—reviled—and it shall be avenged—
Accused of what till now my heart disdained—
Too faithful, though to bitter bondage chained.
Yes, smile!—but he had little cause to sneer,
I was not treacherous then, nor thou too dear:
But he has said it—and the jealous well,—
Those tyrants—teasing—tempting to rebel,—
Deserve the fate their fretting lips foretell.
I never loved—he bought me—somewhat high—
Since with me came a heart he could not buy.
I was a slave unmurmuring; he hath said,
But for his rescue I with thee had fled.
'Twas false thou know'st—but let such Augurs rue,
Their words are omens Insult renders true.

Nor was thy respite granted to my prayer;
This fleeting grace was only to prepare
New torments for thy life, and my despair.
Mine too he threatens; but his dotage still
Would fain reserve me for his lordly will:
When wearier of these fleeting charms and me,
There yawns the sack—and yonder rolls the sea!
What, am I then a toy for dotard's play, □
To wear but till the gilding frets away?
I saw thee—loved thee—owe thee all—would save,
If but to show how grateful is a slave.
But had he not thus menaced fame and life,—
And well he keeps his oaths pronounced in strife—
I still had saved thee—but the Pacha spared:
Now I am all thine own—for all prepared:
Thou lov'st me not—nor know'st—or but the worst.
Alas! this love—that hatred—are the first—
Oh! could'st thou prove my truth, thou would'st not
start, □
Nor fear the fire that lights an Eastern heart;
'Tis now the beacon of thy safety—now
It points within the port a Mainote prow:
But in one chamber, where our path must lead,
There sleeps—he must not wake—the oppressor Seyd!"

"Gulnare—Gulnare—I never felt till now
My abject fortune, withered fame so low:
Seyd is mine enemy; had swept my band
From earth with ruthless but with open hand,
And therefore came I, in my bark of war, □
To smite the smiter with the scimitar;
Such is my weapon—not the secret knife;
Who spares a Woman's seeks not Slumber's life.

Thine saved I gladly, Lady—not for this;
Let me not deem that mercy shown amiss.
Now fare thee well—more peace be with thy breast!
Night wears apace, my last of earthly rest!"

"Rest! rest! by sunrise must thy sinews shake,
And thy limbs writhe around the ready stake,
I heard the order—saw—I will not see— □
If thou wilt perish, I will fall with thee.
My life—my love—my hatred—all below
Are on this cast—Corsair! 'tis but a blow!
Without it flight were idle—how evade
His sure pursuit?—my wrongs too unrepaid,
My youth disgraced—the long, long wasted years,
One blow shall cancel with our future fears;
But since the dagger suits thee less than brand,
I'll try the firmness of a female hand.
The guards are gained—one moment all were o'er— □
Corsair! we meet in safety or no more;
If errs my feeble hand, the morning cloud
Will hover o'er thy scaffold, and my shroud."

IX.

She turned, and vanished ere he could reply,
But his glance followed far with eager eye;
And gathering, as he could, the links that bound
His form, to curl their length, and curb their sound,
Since bar and bolt no more his steps preclude,
He, fast as fettered limbs allow, pursued.
'Twas dark and winding, and he knew not where □

That passage led; nor lamp nor guard was there;
He sees a dusky glimmering—shall he seek
Or shun that ray so indistinct and weak?
Chance guides his steps—a freshness seems to bear
Full on his brow as if from morning air;
He reached an open gallery—on his eye
Gleamed the last star of night, the clearing sky:
Yet scarcely heeded these—another light
From a lone chamber struck upon his sight.
Towards it he moved; a scarcely closing door☐
Revealed the ray within, but nothing more.
With hasty step a figure outward passed,
Then paused, and turned—and paused—'tis She at last!
No poniard in that hand, nor sign of ill—
"Thanks to that softening heart—she could not kill!"
Again he looked, the wildness of her eye
Starts from the day abrupt and fearfully.
She stopped—threw back her dark far-floating hair,
That nearly veiled her face and bosom fair,
As if she late had bent her leaning head☐
Above some object of her doubt or dread.
They meet—upon her brow—unknown—forgot—
Her hurrying hand had left—'twas but a spot—
Its hue was all he saw, and scarce withstood—
Oh! slight but certain pledge of crime—'tis Blood!

X.

He had seen battle—he had brooded lone
O'er promised pangs to sentenced Guilt foreshown;
He had been tempted—chastened—and the chain
Yet on his arms might ever there remain:

But ne'er from strife—captivity—remorse—□
From all his feelings in their inmost force—
So thrilled, so shuddered every creeping vein,
As now they froze before that purple stain.
That spot of blood, that light but guilty streak,
Had banished all the beauty from her cheek!
Blood he had viewed—could view unmoved—but then
It flowed in combat, or was shed by men!

XI.

"'Tis done—he nearly waked—but it is done.
Corsair! he perished—thou art dearly won.
All words would now be vain—away—away!
Our bark is tossing—'tis already day.
The few gained over, now are wholly mine,
And these thy yet surviving band shall join:
Anon my voice shall vindicate my hand,
When once our sail forsakes this hated strand."

XII.

She clapped her hands, and through the gallery pour.
Equipped for flight, her vassals—Greek and Moor;
Silent but quick they stoop, his chains unbind;
Once more his limbs are free as mountain wind!
But on his heavy heart such sadness sate,
As if they there transferred that iron weight.
No words are uttered—at her sign, a door
Reveals the secret passage to the shore;

The city lies behind—they speed, they reach
The glad waves dancing on the yellow beach;
And Conrad following, at her beck, obeyed,
Nor cared he now if rescued or betrayed;
Resistance were as useless as if Seyd
Yet lived to view the doom his ire decreed.

XIII.

Embarked—the sail unfurled—the light breeze blew—
How much had Conrad's memory to review!
Sunk he in contemplation, till the Cape
Where last he anchored reared its giant shape.
Ah!—since that fatal night, though brief the time,
Had swept an age of terror, grief, and crime.
As its far shadow frowned above the mast,
He veiled his face, and sorrowed as he passed;
He thought of all—Gonsalvo and his band,
His fleeting triumph and his failing hand;
He thought on her afar, his lonely bride:□
He turned and saw—Gulnare, the Homicide!"

XIV.

She watched his features till she could not bear
Their freezing aspect and averted air;
And that strange fierceness foreign to her eye
Fell quenched in tears, too late to shed or dry.
She knelt beside him and his hand she pressed,
"Thou may'st forgive though Allah's self detest;

But for that deed of darkness what wert thou?
Reproach me—but not yet—Oh! spare me now!
I am not what I seem—this fearful night☐
My brain bewildered—do not madden quite!
If I had never loved—though less my guilt—
Thou hadst not lived to—hate me—if thou wilt."

XV.

She wrongs his thoughts—they more himself upbraid
Than her—though undesigned—the wretch he made;
But speechless all, deep, dark, and unexprest,
They bleed within that silent cell—his breast.
Still onward, fair the breeze, nor rough the surge,
The blue waves sport around the stern they urge;
Far on the Horizon's verge appears a speck,☐
A spot—a mast—a sail—an arméd deck!
Their little bark her men of watch descry,
And ampler canvass woos the wind from high;
She bears her down majestically near,
Speed on her prow, and terror in her tier;
A flash is seen—the ball beyond her bow
Booms harmless, hissing to the deep below.
Up rose keen Conrad from his silent trance,
A long, long absent gladness in his glance;
"'Tis mine—my blood-red flag again—again—☐
I am not all deserted on the main!"
They own the signal, answer to the hail,
Hoist out the boat at once, and slacken sail.
"'Tis Conrad! Conrad!" shouting from the deck,
Command nor Duty could their transport check!
With light alacrity and gaze of Pride,
They view him mount once more his vessel's side;

A smile relaxing in each rugged face,
Their arms can scarce forbear a rough embrace.
He, half forgetting danger and defeat, □
Returns their greeting as a Chief may greet,
Wrings with a cordial grasp Anselmo's hand,
And feels he yet can conquer and command!

XVI.

These greetings o'er, the feelings that o'erflow,
Yet grieve to win him back without a blow;
They sailed prepared for vengeance—had they known
A woman's hand secured that deed her own,
She were their Queen—less scrupulous are they
Than haughty Conrad how they win their way.
With many an asking smile, and wondering stare, □
They whisper round, and gaze upon Gulnare;
And her, at once above—beneath her sex,
Whom blood appalled not, their regards perplex.
To Conrad turns her faint imploring eye,
She drops her veil, and stands in silence by;
Her arms are meekly folded on that breast,
Which—Conrad safe—to Fate resigned the rest.
Though worse than frenzy could that bosom fill,
Extreme in love or hate, in good or ill,
The worst of crimes had left her Woman still! □

XVII.

This Conrad marked, and felt—ah! could he less?—
Hate of that deed—but grief for her distress;

72

What she has done no tears can wash away,
And Heaven must punish on its angry day:
But—it was done: he knew, whate'er her guilt,
For him that poniard smote, that blood was spilt;
And he was free!—and she for him had given
Her all on earth, and more than all in heaven!
And now he turned him to that dark-eyed slave
Whose brow was bowed beneath the glance he gave, □
Who now seemed changed and humbled, faint and meek,
But varying oft the colour of her cheek
To deeper shades of paleness—all its red
That fearful spot which stained it from the dead!
He took that hand—it trembled—now too late—
So soft in love—so wildly nerved in hate;
He clasped that hand—it trembled—and his own
Had lost its firmness, and his voice its tone.
"Gulnare!"—but she replied not—"dear Gulnare!"
She raised her eye—her only answer there—□
At once she sought and sunk in his embrace:
If he had driven her from that resting-place,
His had been more or less than mortal heart,
But—good or ill—it bade her not depart.
Perchance, but for the bodings of his breast,
His latest virtue then had joined the rest.
Yet even Medora might forgive the kiss
That asked from form so fair no more than this,
The first, the last that Frailty stole from Faith—
To lips where Love had lavished all his breath, □
To lips—whose broken sighs such fragrance fling,
As he had fanned them freshly with his wing!"

XVIII.

73

They gain by twilight's hour their lonely isle.
To them the very rocks appear to smile;
The haven hums with many a cheering sound,
The beacons blaze their wonted stations round,
The boats are darting o'er the curly bay,
And sportive Dolphins bend them through the spray;
Even the hoarse sea-bird's shrill, discordant shriek,
Greets like the welcome of his tuneless beak!□
Beneath each lamp that through its lattice gleams,
Their fancy paints the friends that trim the beams.
Oh! what can sanctify the joys of home,
Like Hope's gay glance from Ocean's troubled foam?

XIX.

The lights are high on beacon and from bower,
And 'midst them Conrad seeks Medora's tower:
He looks in vain—'tis strange—and all remark,
Amid so many, hers alone is dark.
'Tis strange—of yore its welcome never failed,
Nor now, perchance, extinguished—only veiled.□
With the first boat descends he for the shore,
And looks impatient on the lingering oar.
Oh! for a wing beyond the falcon's flight,
To bear him like an arrow to that height!
With the first pause the resting rowers gave,
He waits not—looks not—leaps into the wave,
Strives through the surge, bestrides the beach, and high
Ascends the path familiar to his eye.

He reached his turret door—he paused—no sound
Broke from within; and all was night around. ☐
He knocked, and loudly—footstep nor reply
Announced that any heard or deemed him nigh;
He knocked, but faintly—for his trembling hand
Refused to aid his heavy heart's demand.
The portal opens—'tis a well known face—
But not the form he panted to embrace.
Its lips are silent—twice his own essayed,
And failed to frame the question they delayed;
He snatched the lamp—its light will answer all—
It quits his grasp, expiring in the fall. ☐
He would not wait for that reviving ray—
As soon could he have lingered there for day;
But, glimmering through the dusky corridor,
Another chequers o'er the shadowed floor;
His steps the chamber gain—his eyes behold
All that his heart believed not—yet foretold!

XX.

He turned not—spoke not—sunk not—fixed his look,
And set the anxious frame that lately shook:
He gazed—how long we gaze despite of pain,
And know, but dare not own, we gaze in vain! ☐
In life itself she was so still and fair.
That Death with gentler aspect withered there;
And the cold flowers[28] her colder hand contained,
In that last grasp as tenderly were strained
As if she scarcely felt, but feigned a sleep—
And made it almost mockery yet to weep:
The long dark lashes fringed her lids of snow,

And veiled—Thought shrinks from all that lurked below—
Oh! o'er the eye Death most exerts his might
And hurls the Spirit from her throne of light;☐
Sinks those blue orbs in that long last eclipse,
But spares, as yet, the charm around her lips—
Yet, yet they seem as they forebore to smile,
And wished repose,—but only for a while;
But the white shroud, and each extended tress,
Long, fair—but spread in utter lifelessness,
Which, late the sport of every summer wind,
Escaped the baffled wreath that strove to bind;
These—and the pale pure cheek, became the bier—
But She is nothing—wherefore is he here?☐

XXI.

He asked no question—all were answered now
By the first glance on that still, marble brow.
It was enough—she died—what recked it how?
The love of youth, the hope of better years,
The source of softest wishes, tenderest fears,
The only living thing he could not hate,
Was reft at once—and he deserved his fate,
But did not feel it less;—the Good explore,
For peace, those realms where Guilt can never soar:
The proud, the wayward—who have fixed below☐
Their joy, and find this earth enough for woe,
Lose in that one their all—perchance a mite—
But who in patience parts with all delight?
Full many a stoic eye and aspect stern
Mask hearts where Grief hath little left to learn;
And many a withering thought lies hid, not lost,

76

In smiles that least befit who wear them most.

XXII.

By those, that deepest feel, is ill exprest
The indistinctness of the suffering breast;
Where thousand thoughts begin to end in one, ☐
Which seeks from all the refuge found in none;
No words suffice the secret soul to show,
For Truth denies all eloquence to Woe.
On Conrad's stricken soul Exhaustion prest,
And Stupor almost lulled it into rest;
So feeble now—his mother's softness crept
To those wild eyes, which like an infant's wept:
It was the very weakness of his brain,
Which thus confessed without relieving pain.
None saw his trickling tears—perchance, if seen, ☐
That useless flood of grief had never been:
Nor long they flowed—he dried them to depart,
In helpless—hopeless—brokenness of heart:
The Sun goes forth, but Conrad's day is dim:
And the night cometh—ne'er to pass from him.
There is no darkness like the cloud of mind,
On Grief's vain eye—the blindest of the blind!
Which may not—dare not see—but turns aside
To blackest shade—nor will endure a guide!

XXIII.[33]

His heart was formed for softness—warped to wrong,

Betrayed too early, and beguiled too long; □
Each feeling pure—as falls the dropping dew
Within the grot—like that had hardened too;
Less clear, perchance, its earthly trials passed,
But sunk, and chilled, and petrified at last.
Yet tempests wear, and lightning cleaves the rock;
If such his heart, so shattered it the shock.
There grew one flower beneath its rugged brow,
Though dark the shade—it sheltered—saved till now.
The thunder came—that bolt hath blasted both, □
The Granite's firmness, and the Lily's growth:
The gentle plant hath left no leaf to tell
Its tale, but shrunk and withered where it fell;
And of its cold protector, blacken round
But shivered fragments on the barren ground.

XXIV.

'Tis morn—to venture on his lonely hour
Few dare; though now Anselmo sought his tower.
He was not there, nor seen along the shore;
Ere night, alarmed, their isle is traversed o'er:
Another morn—another bids them seek, □
And shout his name till Echo waxeth weak;
Mount—grotto—cavern—valley searched in vain,
They find on shore a sea-boat's broken chain:
Their hope revives—they follow o'er the main.
'Tis idle all—moons roll on moons away,
And Conrad comes not, came not since that day:
Nor trace nor tidings of his doom declare
Where lives his grief, or perished his despair!
Long mourned his band whom none could mourn beside;

And fair the monument they gave his Bride:□
For him they raise not the recording stone—
His death yet dubious, deeds too widely known;
He left a Corsair's name to other times,
Linked with one virtue, and a thousand crimes.

END.

Made in the USA
Coppell, TX
12 January 2020